Dance Class Etiquette

Secrets for Success From One Dancer to Another

Dance Class Etiquette

Secrets for Success From One Dancer to Another

Melanie Rembrandt

1Win Press® • Los Angeles, CA

Dance Class Etiquette
Secrets for Success From One
Dancer to Another

By Melanie Rembrandt

Copyright © 2017
Melanie Rembrandt
1Win Press™

Printed in the United States of America

ISBN-13: 978-0982695029
ISBN-10: 0982695020

The author and publisher have made every effort to ensure the accuracy of the information contained in this book but assume no responsibility for actions taken as a result of the content. If you see errors, please contact us at www.1winpress.com. Thank you!

This book is dedicated to my mother for her never-ending love, support and sacrifices to help me pursue my lifelong, dance dreams.

I am very grateful and blessed to have you as my mother.

Contents

Introduction

Welcome to the wonderful and exciting world of dance!

Whether you're thinking about taking a class to become a professional dancer, get some exercise, or just have fun, dance will change your life for the better.

After all, dancing offers something for everyone.

It can be a wonderful way to relieve stress, lose extra pounds, meet new people, listen to music, improve memory, and express yourself.

For children, dance can help build confidence, learn discipline, develop coordination skills, discover how to work as a team, and much more.

However, taking a dance class for the first time can be a little scary.

Plus, there are several, "unwritten rules" that you really need to be aware of before stepping into a studio.

As a professional dancer, I have participated in thousands of classes, rehearsals, performances, competitions, events, and more from New York to Hollywood. Today, you can still find me at the dance studio almost every day of the week.

With all of these years of experience, it's time to share some of these "insider" tips with you.

This book explains how to get started, what to expect, and most important, the etiquette to have the best dance class possible!

Are you ready?

What Kind of Dance Class is Right for You?

Your first step is to find an appropriate class for you or your children.

Where do you start?

Well, there are many types and styles of dance out there. And if you want to be a dancer, it's important to find the right instructor and a dance class that fits your specific needs.

With this in mind, here is an outline of some of the more popular dance styles to help guide you in the right direction:

<u>Various Styles of Dance</u>

Ballroom

If you watch some of the shows on television and see dancers whirling around dressed in fancy outfits, you are probably viewing some form of ballroom dancing.

Ballroom involves different styles of partner dancing. Some of the most popular styles include: Cha Cha, Foxtrot, Jive, Lindy Hop, Mambo, Paso Doble, Quickstep, Rumba, Samba, Tango, and Viennese Waltz

This means you have many choices if you want to be a ballroom dancer.

But don't worry.

You don't need to take a partner with you when you start your classes. Ballroom instructors encourage students to dance with different partners in order to become better dancers.

Ballroom is very social, and it's a great way to make new friends, start dancing right away, have fun exercising, and get the opportunity to wear some fabulous outfits!

Hip Hop

Hip Hop is an energetic style of dance that became popular in the early 1990s. With roots in break dancing, Hip Hop dancers can perform as soloists or with a team of people doing various, dance combinations.

And unlike break dancing, Hip Hop choreography usually stays away from long combinations on the floor and includes many sharp, strong and upright movements.

And while these movements tend to flow and appear to be simple, Hip Hop dancers practice their technique and style for many hours.

As a beginning dancer, you will learn basic techniques and build your skills over time.

Jazz

Jazz dance has been around for a long time and was huge in the 1970s and 1980s. Today, you will find all kinds of jazz classes that include: lyrical, contemporary, musical theater, "heels," classic jazz, and combinations of ballet, modern and jazz. The style of jazz you learn really depends on the instructor.

Most jazz classes start with a warm-up and a good stretch. Then, you will do short combinations from one side of the dance studio to the other ("Across the Floor") where you work on turns, leaps and other techniques.

In the last 30-45 minutes of class, you will learn some choreography and then perform it in groups.

Jazz classes provide excellent exercise that include cardio and stretching. Plus, you'll get a mind workout too as you use your brain to learn new steps on a regular basis.

If you are not sure what kind of dance class to try first, look into a jazz class. It is usually more relaxed that a ballet class.

Plus, you can wear comfortable clothes and move to the latest music. It's a lot of fun and will give you a great introduction to the world of dance.

Ballet

Ballet provides the technique for all other dance forms. If you want to increase your flexibility, stamina, coordination, and strength, try a ballet class.

You will start with some exercises at the ballet barre that may include: bending, stretching, arm movements, footwork, and jumping. Then, you will step away from the barre and practice various turns, leaps, choreography, and more on the dance floor.

It takes some time to learn the basics, but in the process, you will get to listen to classical music, improve your posture and even get a brief escape from everyday stressors.

Tap

If you've ever wanted to be a tap dancer, go for it! It's lots of fun and can be a great way to burn calories and express yourself.

In a tap class, you will start with a warm up and then review different steps and combinations. Depending on the instructor, you will only have music for certain portions of the class so you can hear your taps.

Note that it can be frustrating at times to learn how to tap dance, but stick with it. Like anything else, it takes time and practice to be good at it.

Just enjoy the process and making sounds with your feet.

Modern

If you really want to express yourself with dance, check out a modern dance class.

Depending on the instructor, you will start with a warm up and do various movements and choreography based on a combination of ballet, lyrical/contemporary jazz and more.

Note that most of these classes are done with bare feet.

Try Them All!

These are just a few of the many dance styles out there. If you are new to dance, I suggest trying various classes to see what you like best.

You may find that you love several styles and that one technique helps you with another. Or, you may find that you really have a talent for one particular dance form.

Whatever you decide, you have nothing to lose!

You'll learn something new in the process, get some exercise and be able to express yourself through dance movement.

So how do you find the right class? Read on...

How to Find the Right Dance Class in Your Local Area

To begin, look online or in your local phone directory under "Dance Instruction."

Try to find a studio that offers the kind of dance you want in your local area. Next, call the studio and get some answers...

Questions to Ask a New Dance Studio

- What type of dance classes do you offer for someone X number years in age with no experience, little experience, professional level, etc.?

- Do you have any classes that cater to someone just starting out?

- How many people are usually in that class?

- Who teaches that class and what kind of experience do they have?

- Can I watch a class in advance?

- Do you provide parking?

   Keep in mind that most dance studios are usually not in the safest of locations (saving money on rent and class fees), and parking can be a challenge.

- How much are classes? Is the first class free? Are there additional fees I need to know about? (Fees for company membership, shoes, costumes, clothing, travel, missing a class, etc.)

- Do you accept credit cards?

- Are there any dress requirements?

- Where can I find your class schedule and more information online?

By asking these questions, you will know exactly what classes the studio offers and when.

The person answering the phone at the studio will either be the owner, an office assistant, or a scholarship student/intern who is helping out at the desk.

He or she usually knows the schedule, instructors, class fees, etc. and is a great source of information.

Once you call the studios in your local area, asked the above questions and review the schedule, it is now time to decide on a good class at a convenient time for you.

And note that if you have never taken a dance class before, be sure you take a Level I, beginner lesson.

Even if you are an advanced dancer, it is better to start at a new studio taking a lower-level class so you won't have any embarrassing surprises and can check out the situation.

(Maybe you aren't as good as you think you are!)

Also, you will waste money if you attend a class where you need to stay on the side most of the time because you don' know what you're doing. And the other dancers will not appreciate waiting for the instructor to show you each movement either.

It's always a good idea to watch a class that you are considering before actually participating in it.

Many studios allow you to view free of charge.

This is a great way to size up the class, see who you will be dancing with, the skill level needed, what everyone is wearing (including shoe types), the music selections, the instructor's style, etc.

And the dancers will probably want to impress you since you are a new "audience member" … so enjoy their performance!

Now that you know what the class is about, what should you wear?

What to Wear to Dance Class

You may be wondering what you should wear to your new dance class.

Well, to make it easy, it's always best to check out a class in advance to see what other students are wearing. Also, note that many studios have dress-code policies so be sure to ask about this before arriving for class.

Now, if you are in a rush and can't do any research in advance, I have two words of advice for you…

Wear black!

If you want to fit in and look like a dancer, do not wear prints, bright colors or loud clothing to your first class. Choose dance apparel that is black. This is the color of choice for most dancers.

Why?

It's slenderizing and goes with everything. Plus, it hides dirt and perspiration stains. And by wearing black, you can worry less about your clothes and focus more on your dance moves.

And unless you are taking a Hip Hop or Freestyle-type class, stay away from baggy clothing. The instructor will want to see the line of your body when you dance.

Wear something that makes you feel confident and allows you to move.

With this in mind, here are a few, dance apparel suggestions:

Dance Apparel for Women:

- Leggings, yoga pants or long shorts

- Tights with shorts or a short, lightweight ballet skirt

- A leotard (with or without a sports bra as needed)

- A t-shirt or fitted top

- A dark sweatshirt tied around the waist (to use for warmth, sitting/lying on the floor for exercises and as a cover-up)

- Socks/possibly leg warmers

Dance Apparel for Men:

- Running pants or shorts that are easy to move in

- A t-shirt or sweatshirt

- Socks

Remember, you want to focus on your instruction and avoid being distracted (or distracting to others) by your dance apparel choices.

Now, what about dance shoes?

What Shoes Should You Wear to Dance Class?

Starting a new dance class but not sure what dance shoes to wear?

Before making a purchase, or borrowing from a friend, check with the studio first as they may have specific requirements.

If you are going to your very first jazz or Hip Hop class, it is usually o.k. to wear clean running shoes. You can ask the instructor what type of shoes you should buy after class.

However, if you are attending your first ballet class, purchase a pair of ballet slippers. Most ballet instructors will not let you take class if you are not wearing the appropriate shoes.

And if you are planning to take both jazz and ballet classes, you might want to purchase a pair of jazz shoes.

It's not a good idea to wear ballet shoes to a jazz class. They show off the placement of your feet and do not always give you the support you need for various, jazz dance moves.

(Plus, everyone in class will know you are new because only new students wear ballet shoes to jazz class!)

For tap class, you will need to discuss your footwear with the instructor prior to attending class because tap shoes are a necessity. You can always purchase an inexpensive pair of shoes to start, or borrow a pair from a friend.

Obviously, you won't know whether or not you like tap unless you try it with the appropriate tap shoes. If you find that you don't like it, you can always sell your shoes online or donate them to a studio or charity.

When starting out, check your local area for less expensive footwear. Then, once you figure out the shoes you want, you can spend your money on higher quality dance shoes. Your instructor can provide suggestions.

And note that most dancers are always in search of the perfect shoes. Or, they find the perfect fit and wear the shoes until they fall off their feet!

It comes down to a matter of personal choice and comfort.

Still need some help?

Check out this shoe guideline for some of the most popular dance classes...

Dance Class Shoe Guideline

Ballet
Wear ballet flats if possible (avoid running shoes). If you don't have ballet shoes and simply cannot purchase them, where socks to ballet class (but the instructor will probably not be happy!).

Ballroom/Country Western
For introductory classes, wear comfortable shoes that allow you to slide your foot on the floor and move around without slipping.

Women usually wear character shoes, and men wear dance or dress shoes for this type of dance.

Hip Hop/Freestyle
Wear non-marking shoes (no black soles that leave marks on the dance floor) that are comfortable.

Try to wear shoes that will give you support (high tops, cross-trainers, jazz sneakers, etc.). Avoid shoes that are too sticky and don't allow you to slide your foot on the floor.

Jazz
You'll find that most of the dancers in class will wear flat jazz shoes or sneakers depending on the dance floor.

Also, note that most jazz classes begin with dancers going barefoot or wearing socks only (to stretch and work the feet).

Modern
In most modern classes, you will go barefoot or wear socks. Some dancers also wear jazz shoes or special, strapped footwear.

<u>*Tap*</u>

You will need a pair of tap shoes, even if you are taking your first tap dance class. After all, the whole point of this is to make sounds with your feet!

Without tap shoes, it's very difficult to learn what you need to be doing to make the appropriate sounds with your feet.

See if you can borrow a pair of tap shoes from a friend, or buy an inexpensive pair (check online) to use until you figure out whether or not you want to pursue this form of dance.

This is just a quick guideline to give you a better understanding of dance shoes worn in various types of dance classes. It's best to check with the dance studio before making a purchase to avoid wasting time and money.

And what if you have limited funds for apparel?

Dance Apparel and Shoes on a Limited Budget

If you are just starting out in dance, you may be overwhelmed with the apparel and footwear choices available. To save yourself time and money, conduct research in advance.

1. Call the studio.

Ask the instructor or a knowledgeable receptionist/dancer what students wear to class.

They probably have a specific dress code so be sure to get the specifics.

And if you need something that you can't afford, ask if they know of any students who have used shoes or used clothes you can have or borrow.

They may even have some items for you in the lost and found!

2. Visit the studio or their website for class videos.

If you really want a good idea of what the students where to the dance classes you are going to take, visit the studio and look at what the dancers are wearing.

Most studios have a waiting area where you can view classes. Not only will you be able to see the dance techniques taught in a specific class, but you can also see what the students wear while dancing.

Also go to the dance studio's website. Many times, the studios will post videos of their studio and dancers which show choreography, what students wear, technique levels, and more.

3. Start with less expensive choices.

As a new dancer, don't spend a lot on dancewear and shoes until you figure out what works best for you in the classes you like. This way, if you end up disliking a class, you won't lose money on shoes or apparel that you will never wear again!

If you know you need a certain outfit for dance class but have limited funds, visit local thrift shops. Many times, you'll find used dance shoes and almost new, workout clothes.

You won't pay much, and it doesn't really matter because you'll just be working out in the clothes and shoes anyway!

Another way to find used/inexpensive dance shoes and clothing is to look online.

Search for what you need, and see if you can't find used or almost new clothes and shoes in your size and budget-range.

If that doesn't work, call all of the dance studios in your area and ask if they have any used dance shoes you can buy. Also, ask if they have recommendations about where you can get affordable, dance apparel.

4. Test different brands and styles.

There are endless possibilities as new dancewear styles appear regularly.

Just remember that if you try on your shoes or clothes at home, be sure to keep them clean in case you need to exchange or return them.

Great Dance Clothes and Shoes are Waiting for You!

Starting a new dance class can be exciting, but it can also be expensive. To cut down on your nerves, prepare what you are going to wear in advance.

Also, look for clothes and shoes you can afford. Make the effort to contact the dance studio for specifics and assistance, and look online for bargains.

You can find some great outfits and dance shoes to wear to class without ruining your budget.

And most important, you'll fee more confident as you walk into a studio and start your new classes!

But if you're still not sure what to wear, check out this list…

What Not to Wear to Dance Class

We've talked about the appropriate apparel and shoes to wear to a dance class.

Here are some things you may want to *avoid* wearing to class.

What Not to Wear to Dance Class Tip Sheet

1. **Anything worth a lot of money**

   You don't want your stuff to disappear, do you?

   Things get "misplaced" at studios all the time.

2. **Watches, bracelets, earrings, and other jewelry**

   Do you really want to slip on your necklace or accidentally hit someone in the face with your ring or displaced earring?

   Jewelry can easily hurt others, end up on the floor, get lost, and more. It's better to leave it at home.

3. **Bulky clothes that don't show your legs, arms and body placement**

   Trust me. You'll have a better class when the instructor, and you, can actually see what your body is doing.

   Now if it's a Hip Hop/Freestyle class, you can where bulky clothes without a problem.

4. **Hair accessories, glasses or anything else that can fly off when you turn or jump**

   Ensure your hair, accessories and glasses will stay in place throughout the *entire* class.

   Bobby pins, barrettes, hair clips, and more can be dangerous on the dance floor.

5. **Anything you can catch on your feet or arms while moving**

   Have you ever tripped over a long pant-leg or leg warmer? It's not pretty.

6. **Perfume or strong scents**

   I'm sorry. Not everyone wants to inhale your "Pretty Passion Peach Pizzazz Powder" cologne… no matter how great you think it smells!

7. **Body lotion**

   If it gets on the floor, you'll create a slippery mess that is difficult to clean.

8. **Shoes that will mark the dance floor**

   The studio owner will not be happy if your shoes make big, black marks on the dance floor or if you wear your regular, dirty street shoes in class.

   Also, check your tap screws to ensure that they are flat against your tap on the shoe.

   If they stick out, you can damage the dance floor.

9. **Socks, pants or clothes that you want to keep clean**

You're going to be sweating and possibly rolling around on a dirty floor.

Do you really want to have to worry about your clothes getting dirty?

10. **Shirts advertising another dance studio!**

It's not cool to promote another studio while you are taking class somewhere else. Leave shirts from the competition at home!

These are just a few, quick tips.

If you are brand new to dance, this brief list will help you avoid wearing the wrong things to class and start class on a positive note.

In addition, there is something else to think about...

What to Do With Your Hair in Dance Class

If you are taking a dance class for the first time, you need to think about your hair… especially if it is long.

Here are three, hairstyle choices to think about before you step into the studio:

1. Wear it Off Your Face and Pulled Back.

Most dance instructors will ask you pull to your hair up, back and away from your face.

This way, it doesn't get in the way of your training, and the instructor can see your body lines. This is especially true in ballet class.

2. Wear It Down and Work It!

If you are taking a Hip Hop, jazz, modern, or a more casual class, feel free to wear your hair down.

You just want to be able to move without having it get in your way.

And when you where your hair down, it actually becomes part of your movement.

As you'll see in many dance shows and music videos, the dancers whip their hair around and flip their heads to accent certain moves or beats in a dance.

As a professional, you'll learn how to use your hair to add to the choreography and your overall performance… without having it be a distraction.

3. Change Your Hair as Needed.

If you are taking a bunch of different classes with various dance styles, take some hair bands or clips to change your hairstyle accordingly.

For example, you can have it up and away from your face for ballet, let it down for jazz class, and then put it partially up for tap class.

(Just be careful that your ponytail doesn't hit you in the eye when you turn – Ouch!)

By being prepared with appropriate hair accessories and experimenting with different hairstyles, you can change your look appropriately for each class.

Decide What Works Best For You.

If you are a beginning dancer, you may want to wear your hair up all of the time in class so you don't have to think about it.

Over time, you'll figure out what works best for each style of class that you take.

Just remember. Your hair is a part of your body and part of your movement.

If you can get to the point where you forget about your hair while you dance and use it to accent the choreography, you'll significantly improve your overall performance.

Ok. You have the information you need about your apparel, shoes and hair. Now, it's time to prepare for class...

What to Take to Your Dance Classes

When you attend a dance class, there are a few things you need to take with you.

Here's a quick checklist to help you get ready for class:

- **Water**

Many studios have drinking fountains, but have your own bottle of water nearby to stay hydrated. Just ensure that it has a tight cap and won't leak.

- **Snacks**

To keep your energy levels up, it's a good idea to eat a small snack right before class.

And if you are going to be at the studio for a long period of time, take fruit, energy bars, nuts, granola bars, and other nutritious snacks with you.

Then, you can concentrate on class instead of your growling stomach!

And note that most studios do not allow food or drink in the actual studio so be sure to follow the rules.

- **Shoes**

Remember to pack all of the appropriate dance shoes you will need for each class you plan to take.

Wear your street shoes to the studio and change when you get there.

When finished, be sure to put your street shoes back on when you leave. This will help keep your dance shoes clean and in good shape for a longer period of time.

• A Towel

You will probably start "glowing" like a dancer once you warm up so have a towel handy to dab away moisture. Then, you can stay fresher and avoid dripping on the floor or spraying other dancers!

And you may want to use the towel as a cushion for your body for some of the warm-up exercises done on the floor during class, too.

• Tissues

Many times, the movements and turns in many dance classes will cause your nose to start running. Have some tissues handy just in case!

• Sweatshirt/Sweater

After class, have a top to change into that will keep you dry and warm. You can also wear the sweater or sweatshirt at the beginning of class until your muscles warm up and you're ready to dance. Again, check with the instructor first to make sure this is o.k.

• Knee Pads

For more beginning dance classes, you generally will not need knee pads. However, if you are taking a jazz, contemporary or Hip Hop/Freestyle class, you may want to have a pair handy.

Many of the moves in these classes entail going on the floor and getting back up, and the knee pads will help protect your knees.

- **Hair Bands**

For class, you'll want to keep your hair out of your face so you can see what the instructor is doing.

Take some extra hair clips, elastic hair bands, bobby pins, barrettes, or whatever you need to hold your hair in place. And if you lose a hair accessory during class, pick it up off of the floor and have extras ready to go.

- **Checkbook or Cash**

Don't forget to take money to pay for your classes!

Call the dance studio in advance to see how much your will need to pay upfront. Some teachers only accept cash while others will want a check or credit card number upfront.

It's best to arrive at the studio with the appropriate payment early. Then, you can get your payment out of the way and concentrate on your dancing instead.

- **Bandages**

There is a lot of movement going on in class so you never know when you may get a little scratch or bump.

Keep some bandages ready to go. This way, you can protect yourself (and others) from infection quickly and go right back to dancing!

• A Small Screwdriver

What?! Yes, you will need this in case the taps on your tap shoes come loose.

You do not want the screws sticking out and scraping the dance floor. Check the bottom of your taps before class to make sure they are smooth. If a screw is loose or sticks out from the tap, tighten it down with your small screwdriver.

• Personal Bath/Beauty Items

If you need extra deodorant, hair spray, a special brush, or other personal items that will keep your dance class experience "fresh," pack these items for use before or after class.

• Dance Bag

Now that you have everything you need, put it all in a dance bag. This can be a backpack, shoulder bag, duffle bag, or whatever you like.

Just be sure that it holds what you need, is sturdy enough to carry your various dance shoes, and helps to protect your back in some way.

• A Good Attitude!

Finally, think positive! You are prepared and about to embark on the world of dance. Try to do the best you can and avoid frustration.

You are just beginning so give yourself a break. After all, dance is supposed to be fun!

What's next?

What to Do When You Get to The Studio

You've found the studio, decent parking and are thirty minutes early.

Now what?

- **Go to the front desk and explain that you are new and would like to register and pay for a class.**

I suggest buying one "drop-in" class first to see if you like it rather than paying for an entire series.

The desk assistant will probably give you a form to fill out and ask you to sign a liability waiver in case of theft or personal injury.

Then, you generally sign your name on the class list that you intend to take, and pay your fee.

Sign your name quickly, and move to the side of the desk as others will need to sign-in too.

- **Next, check out the studio so you know where everything is.**

Find the dressing room and restroom and see where dancers stretch before class.

Go to the stretching area (it might be in the actual studio if a class is not going on) and do a few stretches to warm-up your body.

- **When you enter the classroom, see what the other students are wearing on their feet.**

Have your shoes ready, but do not put them on yet. Most studios do not want you to wear your dance shoes outside of the dance floor as they get dirty and ruin the dance floor.

And many classes begin in socks or bare feet.

For tap, you'll need to put your shoes on before class starts.

For other classes like jazz and modern, the instructor will give you time to put on your shoes after the warm-up.

- **Place your dance bag in the back or side of the classroom out of the way.**

If possible, keep it within your sight at all times. Thieves can thrive at dance studios, and usually, there are no lockers.

When the instructor walks into the classroom, it's time to begin...

How to Fit In At a New Dance Class

If you are starting a new dance class, it can be a scary thing.

You have to deal with a new teacher, other students you don't know, a different dance floor, and more.

But as a dancer, it's important to take classes from various dance teachers in order to improve your overall skills.

This means that you will be entering new studios throughout life.

This can be challenging, but here are a few tips to help you get through the process.

1. Take a Moment.

Before starting conversations, stay quiet and take in your surroundings.

Are the other students talking in groups?

Is it a quiet or noisy atmosphere?

How are other people dressed and acting?

By taking a few minutes to access your new situation, you'll have a better understanding of how to fit in and feel a little more comfortable.

2. Be Humble.

Whatever you do, do not enter a new studio or class stating that you are better than anyone else there. People will instantly dislike you.

You can learn something from every class you take and every instructor you come across.

If you are really good, it will show in your performance.

And if you discover that your new class is not challenging enough, you can always start looking for another class.

3. Maintain a Positive Attitude.

You will probably be a little nervous, but don't let this get to you.

Remind yourself how lucky you are to take a dance class. After all, there are many people in this world who would love to be where you are right now.

Focus on what the instructor is telling you and learn as much as you can. Then, your surroundings will take a backseat to the learning process.

Go For It!

When you walk into a new dance class, you may have butterflies in your stomach and not be sure what to do.

Take a moment to access your surroundings and then try to act accordingly. It's best to stay quiet about your level of expertise and just learn as much as possible during your class.

The other dancers, and the instructor, will be sizing you up, but don't let this bother you.
Focus on your technique, and try to get the most out of class as possible.

And to help you feel more confident, here are a few tips on what you can expect...

What to Expect in Class

Most classes begin with some kind of warm up with various stretches, cardio and strengthening movements.

Usually, this will be a standard set of movements done at each class you will learn over time for your feet, legs, arms, balance, and more. Follow the instructor carefully as she or he demonstrates each movement.

Do the best that you can, and don't get discouraged!

Remember that you are new and many of the other students have been there a long time.

Try to relax and breathe. Also, remember not to overdo as this can result in injury.

After working at the barre or doing the warm-up, the instructors usually provides a short break and you might hear them call out …

"Shoes!"

Here, you will have just enough time to put on your dance shoes, use the restroom, get a drink of water, stretch more, chat with others, or do anything else that you need to do.

The break usually lasts about five minutes.

Once you have finished putting on your shoes, check to see how slippery the floor is.

This is a good time to step quickly into the rosin box (if there is one) or put some water on the bottom of your shoes so you don' slip.

What is the rosin box?

You may see a mysterious box in the corner of the room. Basically, some studio owners will place yellow, rosin crystals (which come from the sap of pine trees) into this box.

Then, when you step on the crystals, they turn into a white powder that coats the bottom of your shoes.

If you are a new dancer, there are a few things you should know about the rosin box:

- **Step in it only if you want to make your shoes sticky.**

If you accidentally step in the rosin with bare feet or socks, your feet will get sticky.

And I highly advise that you stay out of it when wearing tap shoes. You'll coat your taps, and you will not be able to produce clear, tap sounds.

- **Get in and get out quickly so the next person can use the box.**

When you use the rosin box, step in it with one foot and turn the ball of your foot (for ballet and jazz shoes) to coat that shoe's sole and then do the same with the other.

You do not need to stand there for a long time chatting with friends and rubbing your shoes back and forth. It only takes a few seconds to get the appropriate amount of rosin on your shoes.

And note that you'll probably need to use the rosin several times throughout class so it helps if you can coat your shoes quickly. (Your fellow dancers will appreciate your speed so they can use the box too!)

- **Manage the rosin on your shoes.**

Be aware that as soon as you step out of the box, you will have a lot of rosin on your shoes. And as you walk away from the box, you'll deposit a trail of the rosin behind you all over the dance studio.

Pay attention to where and how you walk so that you don't lose all of the rosin from your shoes and are not getting it on other people... or their property.

- **Avoid tripping on the box.**

Most rosin boxes have a lip on them to keep the rosin in the box.

This makes it very easy to trip in or out of the box, especially when you get a lot of students around the box.

Please remember this. After all, it's no fun to trip over the box and hurt your body... or your pride.

Now, at this point in class, watch what the other students do and where they go next. You are probably ready to go...

Across the Floor

In many classes, it is now time to go "across the floor." This consists of doing different movements from one side of the room to the other, often in pairs. You will usually be working on turns, leaps, kicks, and directional movements.

If you are new, try to evaluate where the end of the line is. You can do this by seeing where the class assistant is standing. This is the person who helped lead the warm up.

The assistant will almost always be at the front of the line. Stand towards the back of the line so you will have time to learn the steps and watch others.

Stay in Your Lane!

When you go across the floor, it is very important to keep moving forward and stay "in your lane."

Follow the person in front of you. If you move out of your lane, you can run into other people and cause injuries.

Sometimes this is difficult because you may be dizzy from a turn, don't know what you are doing or someone else gets in your way.

If you feel like you are moving out of your lane, get back to where you need to be as soon as possible.

Just be sure to keep moving forward as there is a dancer right behind you.

And if a move seems too difficult, don' give up! Remember, some dance steps take a lot of practice to master. Ask for help at the appropriate time, and don't worry about what the others are thinking. They were once where you are now.

When you get to the other side of the room, keep your place in line in order to cross the floor again using the opposite foot to start.

Do not cut in line or change places.

The other dancers will not appreciate this.

Once you get to the other side of the room, the instructor will give another sequence of steps to perform.

Note that you will usually do about five different movements across the floor going both right and then left, depending on the class, time limits and more.

Learning the Combination

When "across the floor" is finished, it's time to learn a dance combination. Once again, try to go towards the back of the room where you can still see the instructor.

If you have trouble seeing the instructor, DO NOT STAND IN THE FRONT ROW.

Instead, go to the second or third row. The first row is reserved for the instructor, assistants, and those who have been attending the class for a long time.

In the front row, you need to know what you are doing. If not, you can move in the wrong direction, possibly injure yourself and others and make some "regulars" very angry.

Focus and try to learn the steps the instructor gives. If you have questions, go ahead and ask.

Just ensure they apply to others and you do not disrupt or monopolize the class by asking too many questions.

You can always talk to the instructor after class, too.

And if you just can't pick-up the choreography, stand in the back of the classroom and watch.

Doing the Combination

Once the instructor has taught the dance, usually he or she will split the room into groups and have each group dance in succession. Remember which group you are in and dance only when your group is called.

When not dancing, stay out of the way of those dancing and go to the back of the room or against the side walls. You can quietly go over the steps there.

Remember to dance in your own personal space and try to go with the flow of those dancing next to you. If you do not know the combination, go to the back of the room.

Again, don't dance in the front unless you know what you are doing. Also, never stand in the front center portion of the floor if the assistant or the instructor is dancing in your group. This is his/her official place to dance, and you should not be there.

Another thing to be aware of is the mirror. If you want to make friends, ensure that the dancers standing behind you can see themselves in the mirror.

If you constantly block others, or stand right next to them, they will not be happy!

After each group performs, usually the other dancers applaud. Be sure to follow what the other students do and encourage each other accordingly.

End of Class

After you dance and cool down, the instructor will thank the class. Then, the students usually applaud the other students and the instructor. If you are in ballet class, thank both the instructor and the pianist, if there is one.

Grab your dance bag, take off your dance shoes and move out of the room quickly. Since other dancers are probably waiting to come in for the next class, you can put on your shoes in the dressing room or hallway.

Also, ensure that you have all of your belongings. Many items look alike so make sure you have your own things.

Congratulations!

You have finished your first class at a new studio and have entered the world of dance!

Hopefully, you have found this information helpful and feel more comfortable starting your dance journey. Now, whether you are a new dancer, or you have been around awhile, the etiquette with attending a dance class remains the same.

Check out the following list to ensure you know these "unwritten rules" and have the most success possible!

And if you need additional assistance, or want to provide feedback, please do not hesitate to contact me.

Have a wonderful day dancing!
Melanie

Dance Class Etiquette

The golden rules to follow in no particular order:

- **Do not wear your street shoes on the dance floor or your dance shoes outside of the studio, if possible.**

  While some studios allow you to walk all over the dance floor in your street shoes, others have very strict rules about this.

  Dance floors are expensive, and in order to keep them from being too slippery, dirty, cracked, dented, etc., this is a must.

- **Never stand in the front and center of class.**

  This is where the instructor or assistant stands. If you know the choreography well and have been in the class for a long time, you can stand behind, or next to, the instructor and assistant.

  If you stand in the front and don't know what you are doing, you will not only be embarrassed, but the other dancers will not appreciate it.

  In the same way, do not stand at the end of the barre in a ballet class if you are new. Here, you cannot watch others for the choreography.

- **Stay in your own space.**

  Do not touch the dancers near you. If the choreography moves to the right, move to the right and vice versa. If someone is a better dancer and moves more than you do, stay out of their way.

This includes staying in your own lane when you go across the floor and moving with the flow.

Do not stand right behind another student in class. This can be very annoying.

And if you accidently touch another dancer, apologize.

With this in mind, do not dance full out (performing to the best of your ability without marking movements) if it is crowded. This can lead to injury. Mind your space at all times.

- **Watch the dancer hierarchy.**

  Most dancers in a class stand in the same space each week. For example, if you see a towel at the ballet barre, that particular space is claimed.

  If you're unsure where to stand, ask if someone else is in that space.

  You can make some enemies fast by standing in the wrong space in class. This may sound silly, but some dancers are very territorial!

- **Stay out of the teacher and assistant's way.**

  The teacher needs space to show choreography, provide tips and feedback and talk to the pianist, if there is one. Give your instructors the space they needs to do their job.

  The assistant is the dancer who helps the instructor with class. This person has probably been taking the class for a long time, knows the instructor well and has worked very hard to become the assistant.

At no time should you dance in front of the assistant or in the assistant's personal space, even if you are a better dancer.

- **If you are not in the group that is dancing, stand as close to the wall as you can.**

  If you need to mark the steps (practicing with small movements), do so quietly and subtly without touching anyone nearby or any items on the floor.

  When you are not dancing, stand out of the way of those dancing. If you are blocking someone else's dance bag, that person cannot get water, tissues, bandages, etc. out of the bag.

  Avoid blocking exits as well.

- **Step in and out of the rosin or water box quickly.**

  If you need to put rosin or water on your shoes so you don't slip, step quickly into the rosin box and get out. Other people are waiting to use it.

- **Leave your jewelry at home.**

  Not only do you risk losing it, but jewelry can get in the way while you dance and even cause injury to you and others.

- **Turn your phone off.**

  This is a big No-No at most studios. If your cell phone rings during class, it can be embarrassing.

  Plus, you will probably get a dirty look from the instructor and those in class.

- **Wear your hair away from your face in ballet class.**

  Many studios have specific rules about your hair. Check before taking a class.

  These rules are in place so that the instructor can see your body lines and your hair doesn't get in your face when you dance and turn.

  With this in mind, secure any hair clips, bands, barrettes, etc. so they will not fly out of your hair when you move.

  It's not only distracting to have your hair in your eyes when you dance, but if a bobby pin, hair clip, barrette, etc. gets on the dance floor, another dancer can slip on it. This can be dangerous.

- **Do not touch anything that does not belong to you.**

  This includes moving a towel on the barre, leaning on clothing or standing/sitting on dance bags. You also need to avoid hanging or leaning on the ballet barre or wall unless you are doing a specific stretch.

- **Do not eat or drink in the studio.**

  This is a strict rules in most dance studios for safety reasons. Not only can you choke on a piece of food or gum, it can cause a mess on the dance floor and shoes.

  The same goes for drinks. Stick to a bottle of water.

  Usually, you can take a bottle of water into the studio or have it on the side of the room. However, be sure to check the studio rules before entering the dance floor. Some studios do not allow any type of beverage or food onto the dance floor.

Also, be sure to keep any snacks outside of the studio and clean up after yourself.

- **Watch your water bottle.**

  If you take your water bottle into the studio, make sure you secure the lid carefully.

  It can spill easily with students moving around, and you don't want to spend your time mopping up the floor!

- **Be quiet when the instructor is speaking or giving a correction.**

  You can learn from what he or she tells other students.

- **Keep your tap shoes quiet when not dancing.**

  If you wear tap shoes, keep them quiet unless you are supposed to be dancing.

  It is really annoying if the instructor is trying to show a step, and all you hear is someone else tapping.

- **Take notes.**

  While most studies ban the use of cameras and videos, it's important to document what you learn. After class, write notes for what you learned.

  If instructors do the same choreography later, they will expect you to remember it.

And if you receive corrections, write them down as well so that the instructor does not need to keep reminding you.

This will also help you learn techniques faster.

- **Arrive at the studio early.**

  It's smart to arrive at least 30 minutes prior to your dance class so you can warm up and prepare accordingly.

  If you are late, ask the instructor if it's o.k. to enter the classroom. Many studios are very strict about this.

  The reason for this is that if you are too late, you are not only disrupting the class, but you risk getting injured from not being warmed up appropriately.

  It is also disrespectful to be late.

  And if you need to sign-in for class, do so quickly and get out of the way. Other people need to sign-in too!

- **Follow instructions.**

  It's important to listen to your instructors at all times. They will tell you when it's o.k. to take a break, get a drink of water, and more.

  If you need to leave the class for an emergency, let the instructor know at the most appropriate time possible and leave quietly.

- **Pay for your classes on time.**

  Try to keep track of your classes and make new payments when they are due.

Some studios will stop classes and call out students who have not paid accordingly.

This is not only embarrassing, but it disrupts the class too.

- **Do the best you can.**

  If you are having a difficult time with choreography, stand in the back and try your best. It is rude to just pick up and leave so try to learn as much as you can, stay out of the way of other dancers and keep a positive attitude.

- **Do not give corrections to other dancers.**

  Only the instructor is allowed to give corrections to other students. Refrain from doing so at all cost.

- **Keep your questions to a minimum.**

  While it's fine to ask questions about a particular movement, do not ask too many questions.

  If you have a question that only applies to you, wait until after class to ask the instructor.

  In a beginning class, it's usually fine to ask many questions. However, if you are taking a more advanced class, keep your questions to a minimum and ensure they apply to everyone in class.

  Otherwise, you will slow down the class, and your fellow dancers will not appreciate all of your interruptions.

- **Dress appropriately.**

  Know what the dress code is for your class in advance. If you are allowed to wear whatever you want, be sure it is appropriate and that your clothes fit accordingly and are not distracting.

- **Say "Thank You."**

  When you receive a correction from instructors, thank them. At the end of some classes, you'll simply applaud the instructor.

  At others, you actually go up to the instructor (and pianist if there is one) and personally thank him or her. Follow what the other students do.

- **Show respect.**

  When you're not sure what to do, look around and try to do the right thing. Show respect for those around you and act accordingly.

  Try to avoid yawning, sitting on the floor or being confrontational. Always be open to learning with a positive attitude.

  Know that the dance world is small, and talk travels quickly.

- **Be supportive of other dancers.**

  If you can't say anything nice, don't say anything at all. Period.

By following these simple rules, you will have a better, dance class experience now and in years ahead!

About The Author

Melanie Rembrandt has been dancing since the age of three, when she was the worst one in her class. But, she loved it so much that she spent thousands of hours at the studio and practicing in her basement.

Over time, she got better and started to win dance competitions and roles in numerous shows. In fact, she won the "Miss Teenage America" talent competition – beating more than 8,000 teenagers nationwide.

Her success and love for dance led her to attend UCLA's prestigious School of Theater, Film and Television where she graduated magna cum laude.

After many auditions, rehearsals and classes, she got her big break at an open call for "Gypsy," winning a part over hundreds of other experienced dancers and actors.

Today, as a member of SAG-AFTRA and Actors' Equity, Melanie has performed in hundreds of musical theater, film and television shows.

And you can usually find this busy dancer and author taking dance class or helping others via her presentations, books and various businesses.

To reach Melanie and learn more about dance, visit www.dancefullout.com.

Questions and comments about this book may be sent to:

Dance Full Out®
800 S. Pacific Coast Highway, Ste. #8-280
Redondo Beach, CA 90277
www.dancefullout.com

www.ingramcontent.com/pod-product-compliance
Lightning Source LLC
Chambersburg PA
CBHW060623030426
42337CB00018B/3163